10 x POP

£4.95
>> less than 50p a song

10 x Ultimate Pop Hits
PVG

Published by
Wise Publications
8/9 Frith Street, London,
W1D 3JB, England.

Exclusive distributors:
Music Sales Limited
Distribution Centre,
Newmarket Road,
Bury St Edmunds, Suffolk,
IP33 3YB, England.

Music Sales Pty Limited
120 Rothschild Avenue, Rosebery,
NSW 2018, Australia.

Order No. AM985545
ISBN 1-84609-559-X

www.musicsales.com

call my name CHARLOTTE CHURCH 2

filthy/gorgeous SCISSOR SISTERS 8

good people JACK JOHNSON 14

oops!... i did it again BRITNEY SPEARS 22

freak like me SUGABABES 28

i'm outta love ANASTACIA 33

suddenly i see KT TUNSTALL 40

survivor DESTINY'S CHILD 47

this love MAROON 5 54

tripping ROBBIE WILLIAMS 59

WISE PUBLICATIONS
part of The Music Sales Group

London / New York / Paris / Sydney / Copenhagen / Berlin / Madrid / Tokyo

Call My Name

Words & Music by Charlotte Church, Wayne Hector & Francis White

Both___ ends of the can-dle burnt___ by the flame,_ yeah, I

love it when you call my name,_____ n - n - name!___

To Coda ⊕

I like the sound of your shirt rip - ping,___ my will slip-ping

4

5

you know_ me._____ But I love it when you call my name,_

_ I love it when you call my name._ Both_ ends of the can-dle burnt_

1.
_ by the flame,_ yeah, I love it when you call my name._____ But I

2.
love it when you call my name,_____ n - n - name!__

Filthy/Gorgeous

Words & Music by Jason Sellards, Scott Hoffman & Ana Lynch

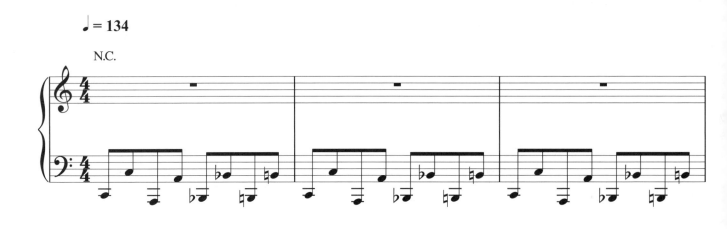

peo - ple that you meet_ want to op - en you up__ like Christ - mas;__
work_ for the man,_ but your big - gest mon - ey - mak - er's flac - cid;__

you got - ta wrap your_ fuz - zy with a big red bow, ain't
you got - ta keep your shit to - ge - ther with your feet on the ground, there ain't

no some bitch gon - na treat me like a ho. I'm a class - y hon - ey, kiss - y hug - gy,
no one gon - na lis - ten if you have - n't made a sound. You're an a - cid junk - ie, col - lege flunk - y,

9

lovey dovey ghetto princess! / dirty puppy daddy bastard! 'Cos you're filthy, ooh, and I'm gorgeous. 'Cos you're filthy, ooh, and I'm gorgeous. You're disgusting,

ooh,__ and you're nas - ty; and you can

grab me, ooh,__ 'cos you're nas - ty.

To Coda ⊕

1.

2.

N.C.

2. When you're (Vocoder) 'Cos you're

You can grab me, ooh,____ 'cos you're

nas - ty.

N.C. *D.S. al Coda*

'Cos you're

Coda

C⁵   B♭⁵   A♭⁵   F⁵   N.C.

nas - ty.

13

Good People

Words & Music by Jack Johnson

one, two, now what__ you gon - na do? Bad news, mis - used, gim - me some truth, you got

too much to loose. Who's side are we on? Ev - 'ry day,__ ev - 'ry way,__ O. K., what - e - ver you say.__

Run the re - so - lute but in the mood to o - bey.__ Sta - tion to sta - tion, de - sens - it -

- i - zing the na - tion. Go - ing, go - ing gone.

21

Oops!...I Did It Again

Words & Music by Max Martin & Rami

23

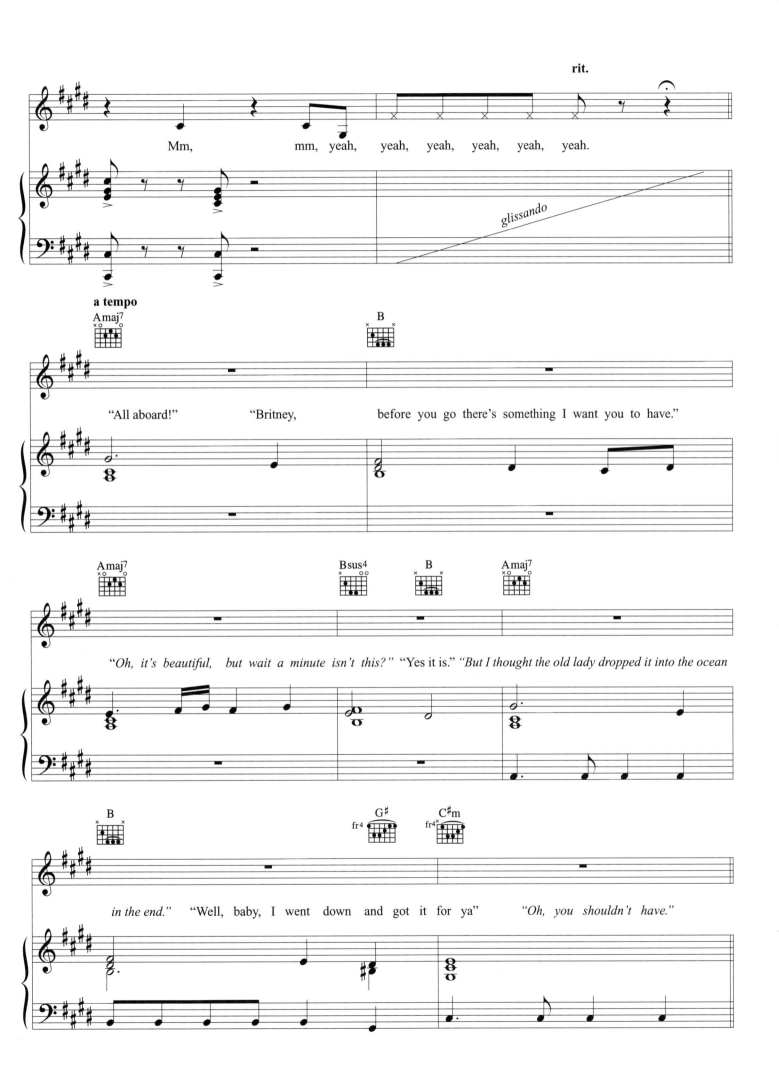

rit.

Mm,   mm, yeah, yeah, yeah, yeah, yeah, yeah.

glissando

a tempo

Amaj7   B

"All aboard!"   "Britney,   before you go there's something I want you to have."

Amaj7   Bsus4   B   Amaj7

"Oh, it's beautiful,   but wait a minute isn't this?" "Yes it is." *"But I thought the old lady dropped it into the ocean*

B   fr4 G#   fr4 C#m

in the end." "Well, baby, I went down and got it for ya"   *"Oh, you shouldn't have."*

25

Oops! I did it a-gain_____ to your heart._____ Got-a lost

in this game, oh ba - by._____ Oops! You

think that I'm sent_____ from a-bove._____ I'm not that in-no-cent.

Oops! I did it a - gain._____ I've played with your heart,_____

Verse 2:
You see my problem is this;
I'm dreaming away,
Wishing that heroes; they truly exist.
I cry, watching the days,
Can't you see? I'm a fool in so many ways.
But to lose all my senses;
That is just so typically me.

Oops! I did it again *etc.*

27

Freak Like Me

Words & Music by Gary Numan, Eugene Hanes, Marc Valentine,
Loren Hill, William Collins, George Clinton & Gary Cooper

that kind of man 'cos I'm that kind of girl, I've got a
frea-ky sec-ret, ev-'ry-bo-dy sing 'cos we don't give a damn a-bout a thing. 'Cos I will be a
freak un-til the day, un-til the dawn. And we can...
(pump) all through the night till the ear-ly morn. Come on and I will

Verse 2
Boy you're moving kind of slow,
You gotta keep it up, now there you go.
That's just one thing that a man must do.
I'm packing all the flavours you need,
I got you shook up on your knees,
'Cos it's all about the dog in me.

I wanna freak in the morning *etc.*

I'm Outta Love

Words & Music by Anastacia, Sam Watters & Louis Biancaniello

Verse 2:
Said how many times
Have I tried to turn this love around?
But every time,
You just let me down.
Come on, be a man about it,
You'll survive.
Sure that you can work it out alright,
Tell me; yesterday, did you know,
I'd be the one to let you go?
And you know...

I'm outta love *etc.*

Suddenly I See

Words & Music by KT Tunstall

I can see her eyes look-ing from a page in a ma-ga-zine. She makes_ me feel_ like I could be a tow - er. Big_ strong tow - er, yeah._ The pow - er to be,_ the pow - er to give, the pow - er to see,_ yeah, yeah._ (Sud - den - ly I

Survivor

Words & Music by Beyonce Knowles, Anthony Dent & Matthew Knowles

broke without — you, but I'm richer. You thought that I'd be sad without — you, I laugh harder. Thought I wouldn't

grow without — you, now I'm wiser. Thought that I'd be helpless with-out you, but I'm smarter, You thought that I'd be

stressed with-out—you, but I'm chill-in'. You thought I would-n't sell with-out—you, sold nine million. I'm a sur-

-vi - vor, I'm not gon' give up. I'm not gon' stop, (what) I'm gon' work hard - er. I'm a sur-

49

Bring much success, no stress and lots of happiness. I'm bet-ter than that, I'm not gon' blast you on the ra-di-o. I'm

bet-ter than that,___ I'm not gon' lie on you___ and your fam-i-ly too. I'm

bet-ter than that,___ I'm not gon' hate on you___ in the ma-ga-zines. I'm

bet-ter than that. I'm not gon' com-pro-mise my Chris-ti-a-ni-ty. I'm

50

Verse 2:
Thought I couldn't breathe without you, I'm inhalin'
Thought I couldn't see without you, perfect vision
Thought I couldn't last without you, but I'm lastin'
Thought that I would die without you, but I'm livin'
Thought that I would fail without you, but I'm on top
Thought that it would be over by now, but it won't stop
Thought that I would self-destruct, but I'm still here
Even in my years to come, I'm still gonna be here.

I'm a survivor *etc.*

This Love

Words & Music by Adam Levine, James Valentine, Jesse Carmichael,
Mickey Madden & Ryan Dusick

1. I was__ so high__ I did__ not re-cog-nise__ the fire__ burn-ing
2. I tried__ my best__ to feed__ her ap-pe-tite,__ to keep her com-ing

Tripping

Words & Music by Robbie Williams & Stephen Duffy